the lily of the field
and
the bird of the air

THE LILY OF THE FIELD

AND

THE BIRD OF THE AIR

Three Godly Discourses

SØREN KIERKEGAARD

Translated and with an introduction
by Bruce H. Kirmmse

PRINCETON UNIVERSITY PRESS
Princeton and Oxford

Copyright © 2016 by Princeton University Press
Published by Princeton University Press,
41 William Street, Princeton, New Jersey 08540
In the United Kingdom: Princeton University Press,
6 Oxford Street, Woodstock, Oxfordshire OX20 1TR

press.princeton.edu

Cover photograph: *Pink Lilies (Liliaceae), Some in Bloom,
Others Wilting.* Courtesy of David Axelbank / Gallery Stock

Second printing, and first paperback printing, 2018

Paper ISBN 978-0-691-18083-0

The Library of Congress has cataloged the cloth edition
as follows:

Names: Kierkegaard, Søren, 1813–1855.
Title: The lily of the field and the bird of the air : three godly
discourses / Søren Kierkegaard ; translated and with an
introduction by Bruce H. Kirmmse.
Other titles: Lilien paa marken og fuglen under himlen. English
Description: Princeton, NJ : Princeton University Press, 2016.
Identifiers: LCCN 2015035995 | ISBN 9780691170473
(hardback : alk. paper)
Subjects: LCSH: Christian life—Lutheran authors. |
Philosophy, Danish.
Classification: LCC BV4505 .K45513 2016 |
DDC 242—dc23 LC record available at
http://lccn.loc.gov/2015035995

British Library Cataloging-in-Publication Data is available

This book has been composed in Adobe Caslon Pro

Printed on acid-free paper. ∞

Printed in the United States of America

3 5 7 9 10 8 6 4 2

CONTENTS

INTRODUCTION
Letting Nature Point beyond Nature

Bruce H. Kirmmse

Søren Kierkegaard is perhaps most known for his pseudonymous works, including *Either/Or*, *Fear and Trembling*, and *The Sickness unto Death*, all of which have a clear (if not always immediately visible) religious undercurrent. But he also wrote a good many non-pseudonymous, overtly religious works, most of which consisted of what he called "discourses" (because he was not ordained, he felt it inappropriate to label them "sermons"). He made frequent use of Matthew 6:24–34, a portion of the Sermon on the Mount, in which Jesus tells his followers to let go of earthly concerns by considering the lilies of the field and the birds of the air. This is a passage that can be interpreted in various ways and put to many different uses, and Kierkegaard had done so on numerous occasions prior to publishing the present work, *The Lily of the Field and the Bird of the Air: Three Godly Discourses*, in April 1849.[1] For example, the second part of *Upbuilding Discourses in Various Spirits*, which Kierkegaard had published in March 1847, consisted of three discourses collectively titled "What We Learn from the Lilies of the Field and the Birds of the Air," and the first part of *Christian Discourses*, published in April 1848, consisted of seven discourses that were also based on the lilies and the birds of Matthew's gospel.

Kierkegaard delivered the manuscript of *The Lily of the Field and the Bird of the Air* to Bianco Luno's Printing House in Copenhagen on April 17, 1849, and by May 9, the fifty-one pages that constitute the first edition had been typeset; proofread three times by Kierkegaard and his secretary, Israel Levin; printed and bound in printed paper covers; and was ready to be sent to bookshops. On May 14, it was advertised in the newspaper *Adresseavisen* as available for purchase from the publisher, university bookseller C. A. Reitzel.[2]

Just over a year earlier, on March 6, 1848, Kierkegaard had delivered the manuscript of *Christian*

Discourses to Bianco Luno. *Christian Discourses* was a composite work consisting of four separate parts, and, as noted above, the first part, "The Cares of the Pagans," builds on Matthew 6:24–34 and makes much use of the lily and the bird, who serve as our teachers with respect to "cares." *Christian Discourses* was ready at the printer's on April 13, 1848, and would become available for purchase on April 25. Kierkegaard undoubtedly had his own copies of the book before Easter Sunday (April 23), and on that same Easter Sunday, he wrote a journal entry, under the heading "New Discourses on the Lilies and the Birds," containing an idea for three additional discourses.[3] Presumably, the circumstance that *Christian Discourses*, which was to go on sale two days later, had made much use of the lily and the bird is what inspired Kierkegaard to think of producing a "new" set of discourses on the lilies and the birds, which in the event became the work in the present volume.

Kierkegaard also had a good deal of other work on his desk in 1848. He had begun writing *The Sickness unto Death* as early as February or

March of that year, and he finished it in mid-May.[4] He put that book aside, however, and it did not appear until July 30, 1849, that is, two and a half months after he published *The Lily of the Field and the Bird of the Air*. In the course of the summer and autumn of 1848 and into the early months of 1849, Kierkegaard wrote the three pieces that he would eventually consolidate as *Practice in Christianity*, which, however, did not appear in print until September 25, 1850.[5] In addition to all this, during the summer and autumn of 1848, Kierkegaard wrote *The Point of View for My Work as an Author* (posthumously published in 1859) as well as several shorter pieces—he called them "notes"—also concerning his work and his development as an author. A reworked portion of these pieces eventually coalesced into "The Accounting," which formed the principal part of the little book *On My Work as an Author*, which Kierkegaard published in 1851.

Kierkegaard seems to have returned to the idea for "new discourses on the lily and the bird" in March 1849, and the writing then proceeded very quickly. Thus, the next month, April 1849, when *The Lily of the Field and the Bird of the Air* was already in the process of publication, Kierkegaard reflected on the difficulties he had experienced during the previous year in connection with the above-mentioned autobiographical "notes" concerning his life and work:

> It was divine fortune that I didn't do it, didn't publish "the notes," or that God didn't permit it to happen....
>
> The degree to which it is God who directs the whole thing is clearest to me from the fact that the discourses on the lily and the bird were produced at that time—and that was just what I needed. God be praised! Without fighting with anybody and without speaking about myself, I said much of what needs to be said, but movingly, mildly, upliftingly.[6]

After the publication of the present work in April 1849, Kierkegaard was by no means finished with considering the many ways in which the lily and the bird could be understood. Kierkegaard is a demanding writer and thinker. He never permits the reader to ease up on the oars and drift in an intellectual, ethical, or spiritual sense. Despite his willingness to use natural imagery to make a point, Kierkegaard is never sentimental and never lets his reader off the hook. In a journal entry written only a year and a half after the publication of the present work, he voiced his agreement with Pascal, that "only rarely and for few does God step forth from his concealment in nature's secrecy"[7]—and a reader might thus hope that difficulties will recede when the lily and bird in fact make an appearance. But Kierkegaard is never lax in this way. For Kierkegaard, Christianity is a moral and spiritual exercise that has the ultimate purpose of teaching human beings their imperfection, their weakness and selfishness, in the face of the perfection, majesty, and absolute otherness of God. To this end, in Kierkegaard's theology the selfless suffering of Jesus Christ is meant to confront us human beings with our radical inadequacy and our selfishness, humbling us in our need for grace.

But, as Kierkegaard explains in another entry from the journal just cited, this is a not a very cheerful-sounding message, so human beings have domesticated Christianity and invented something else called "established Christendom," which "dates from the moment the festival of Christmas was declared to be the supreme festival in the 4th century. The Savior of the world was now a child."[8] To be saved by a child, Kierkegaard explains, is an excellent way to relax the spiritual and moral tension, for with a cute infant Jesus the believer is not confronted with any selfless suffering, and hence with no moral or spiritual challenge. And, to return to the present theme—the lily and the bird—Kierkegaard goes on to state, quite archly, that people prefer the baby Jesus to the suffering Christ because "to be saved by a child is something like 'learning' from the lily and the bird, which people also prefer to an actual 'teacher.'"[9] So, is Kierkegaard abandoning the lily and the bird here? By no means. But this journal entry should serve to remind the reader that Kierkegaard was a tough-minded theologian who never gives his reader a free ride.

In 1850, about a year after he published this simple-*seeming* masterpiece, *The Lily of the Field and the Bird of the Air*, Kierkegaard jotted the following remark in his journal: "The matter is quite simple: The situation is far from being confused enough for people to make proper use of me."[10] But now, in the twenty-first century, it seems that the situation may have become sufficiently confused for us to "make proper use" of Kierkegaard. Nonetheless, there may be an air of something difficult or slightly forbidding in the reputation that surrounds the famous Danish thinker. So for a new reader of Søren Kierkegaard it might be useful to outline a few parallels to—and significant differences from—one of his contemporaries, a figure perhaps more familiar to Americans, Henry David Thoreau.

The brief lives of these two loners, Kierkegaard (1813–1855, died at age forty-two) and Thoreau (1817–1862, died at age forty-four), coincided not only in *when* they were lived, but also in *how* they were lived. Both were second-generation Romantics who did not fit in with the movements with which they were associated: Kierkegaard was the misfit of the Danish Golden Age; Thoreau the oddball among the Transcendentalists. But both had been profoundly influenced by Romanticism's discovery of the *self* and thus are among the most famous (and inveterate) journal-keepers known to literature.

Both Kierkegaard and Thoreau had a deep sense that their times—the beginning of the modern age in the first half of the nineteenth century, which was marked by the triumph of popular sovereignty, the advent of mass circulation newspapers, and the rise of factories, railroads, and telegraphy (the first form of instantaneous communication)—were out of joint. And not just the times, but the lives being lived by most people were similarly out of joint. Quite remarkably, both men simultaneously hit upon an identical characterization of this malaise: At about the same time that Thoreau famously remarked (in *Walden*) that "the mass of men lead lives of quiet desperation,"[11] Kierkegaard repeatedly wrote of "*stille Fortvivlelse*" (quiet desperation, or silent despair), a phrase that makes at least half a dozen appearances, both in his journals and in his published work, between 1839 and 1852. Such was

Kierkegaard's and Thoreau's description of their age, though they meant quite different things by their apparently similar diagnoses.

Both Kierkegaard and Thoreau were indefatigable *walkers*. Thoreau walked everywhere it was possible to walk, and, second only to "Civil Disobedience," his most-read essay was surely "Walking," which he delivered frequently in oral form and which was published after his death. Thoreau begins his essay by humorously celebrating those who have understood

> the art of Walking, that is, of taking walks, who had a genius, so to speak, for *sauntering*, which word is beautifully derived "from idle people who roved about the country, in the Middle Ages, and asked charity, under the pretense of going *à la Sainte Terre*," to the Holy Land.... Some, however, would derive the word from *sans terre*, without land or a home, which, therefore, in the good sense, will mean, having no particular home, but equally at home everywhere. For this is the secret of successful sauntering. He who sits still in a

house all the time may be the greatest vagrant of all.[12]

It is particularly for solitary and independent souls that Thoreau recommends walking: "If you are ready to leave father and mother, and brother and sister, and wife and child and friends, and never see them again,—if you have paid your debts, and made your will, and settled all your affairs, and are a free man, then you are ready for a walk."[13]

Kierkegaard, too, was famously peripatetic, and as a twenty-four-year-old young man he echoed Thoreau's sentiments quite closely, expressing pity "for those who have never felt nostalgia for some unknown, remote something, never [felt] the profundity of being nothing at all, of strolling out of Nørreport with four shillings in your pocket and a slender cane in hand."[14] Kierkegaard was constantly on the move, walking everywhere in and around Copenhagen, talking first with one person, then another. When his sister-in-law was bedridden with depression, Kierkegaard wrote to encourage her, "Above all, do not lose your desire to walk … every day I walk myself into a

state of well-being and walk away from every ill-
ness; I have walked myself into my best thoughts,
and I know of no thought so burdensome that
one cannot walk away from it."[15]

And as both Kierkegaard and Thoreau were
such avid walkers, it is not surprising that both
were also careful observers of the natural world.
Thoreau's interest in every aspect of nature is
widely known, of course, but Kierkegaard, too,
was a bit of a naturalist. In 1850, when his
nephew Henrik Lund was stationed in Odense
during the war over Schleswig-Holstein, Kierkegaard wrote him a letter, now lost, in which he
asked, not necessarily about the war, but quite
definitely about bird life in the region around
Odense. We know of Kierkegaard's inquiry from
Lund's reply to his Uncle Søren, in which Lund
provided details about various species, including
jackdaws, owls, and martins.

Perhaps as a subcategory of this curiosity
about the natural world, both Thoreau and Kierkegaard were also *meteorologists* of sorts—though
of very *different* sorts, and thus for very different ends. Thoreau, for example, declared himself

"self-appointed inspector of snowstorms."[16] Kierkegaard, on the other hand, not immodestly declared himself a "genius," noting that "geniuses are like thunderstorms: they go against the wind, terrify people, and cleanse the air."[17] Thoreau was fascinated by the natural world as such, whereas Kierkegaard's references to the natural world served principally to propel him into a world more real, but unseen.

Although both writers were keen observers of nature, both used their observations to point to an ultimate reality beyond what is merely apparent. Unsurprisingly, both were deeply influenced by Greek philosophy, especially Plato, and by German idealism. Thus Thoreau: "It is well to have some water in your neighborhood, to give buoyancy to and float the earth. One value even of the smallest well is, that when you look into it you see that earth is not continent but insular."[18] And Kierkegaard: "Why I so much prefer autumn to spring is that in the autumn one looks at heaven—in the spring at the earth."[19] Here, again, although both writers make use of nature in referring to what is beyond the immediately visible, we can see the contrast between Thoreau's delight at earthly insularity and Kierkegaard's focus not on what is empirical, on what is earthly, but on something beyond nature, on what cannot actually be seen—a focus not on the earth, but on "heaven."

Thus, as a "naturalist," Kierkegaard *made use* of nature far more radically than did Thoreau, allowing the lily and the bird to point to something invisible but real that lay beyond the visible world—and indeed, what Kierkegaard pointed to was far more real than what is merely visible. As noted, he had made use of these natural objects, the lily and the bird, several times before, but never so trenchantly and brilliantly as in the pieces in the present book. The use Kierkegaard made of the natural world—like the use he requires his *readers* to make of the natural world—was precisely the opposite of the pantheistic religion of nature so common among his contemporaries and our own. Kierkegaard insisted on the absolute transcendence of God, and he held that human beings, unlike other beings, are not only capable of relating to this radically transcendent God, but are fragmentary, incompletely realized, beings, unless they do so.

In the opening pages of his masterwork, *The Sickness unto Death*—which brackets *The Lily of the Field and the Bird of the Air*, having been written shortly before those discourses were written, and published shortly after their appearance— Kierkegaard argues that a human being, or a self, is "spirit," and that spirit is a synthesis of the infinite and the finite, of the temporal and the eternal, of freedom and necessity. But a human being, Kierkegaard insists, is more than this: a human being is not merely a synthesis of opposed properties such as those just mentioned—a synthesis that he calls a "relation"—but is in fact a relation that "relates itself to itself," and it is this self-relating relation that is the self. Such a self-relating relation is not a given entity, but a *capacity*: the self is *that* this relation can relate itself to itself— that is, possess self-consciousness. Furthermore, even at this point, the self, as Kierkegaard tells us, "is still not a self," because such a self-conscious, self-relating relation "must either have established itself or have been established by another."[20] And

Kierkegaard, as a matter of belief, holds that the human self has indeed been "established by another," namely by the transcendent God of biblical tradition. Thus, Kierkegaard's complete definition of the human self is "a relation that relates itself to itself and in relating itself to itself relates itself to another," that is, to "the power that established it."[21]

For Kierkegaard, then, the human self, human self-consciousness, involves relating *both* to the elements of the synthesis within the self *and* to God. As he writes in a journal entry from early 1852—about three years after the composition of *The Lily of the Field and the Bird of the Air*—human beings are characterized by possessing a "double-essence," a status that differentiates us radically from other created beings, and specifically from lilies and birds. This entry demonstrates that Kierkegaard had not forgotten his beloved lilies and birds, and he invokes these creatures precisely in order to draw a clear line between a straightforward, unchallenging veneration of "nature," on the one hand, and, on the other hand, a relation to God that is appropriate for human beings:

"But," I hear someone say, "is this God I am to love, is it not the God, the same God, who has created the whole of this splendid world? How, then, could he be opposed to my loving it, rejoicing in it, in his gifts? Do not the sparrow and the lily and all of nature take joy in it in the same way?" To this Christianity must reply: "Rubbish. First of all, do you really know that the lily and the sparrow rejoice? Next, if you are able to rejoice in the same way as the sparrow and the lily, go right ahead. But you cannot. For the sparrow and the lily and all of the life of nature are simple; the sparrow is no double-essence, no synthesis— no either/or exists for it…. Only the human being is a double-essence."[22]

And in yet another journal entry, this one from late in 1852, Kierkegaard once again touches on the lily and the bird—actually, only the bird, and specifically, "the sparrow"—in order to underscore the absolute, qualitative gulf that separates mere "pagan" material delight in the created world from the ineffable blessedness of the Christian relation to "God's majesty," a majesty so utterly removed from ordinary human, sensate categories that the human relation to it can only be one of "suffering":

> In paganism, God's majesty is merely the superlative of human majesty, and its distinguishing mark is therefore straightforward.
>
> Only in Christianity does God's majesty come to be properly majesty, qualitatively different from what it is to be human, a paradoxical majesty that is therefore recognizable by suffering.
>
> Take the same matter in a different way. Think the thought: God's confiding, or sharing confidence with God. If the content of the confidence is that all the happiness and good fortune that comes a person's way is from God, then there is no relationship of spirit—thus there is no confidence with God in the highest sense, because God is spirit.
>
> No, when that which comes from God is suffering—but then what is confided is that

this suffering signifies God's love, look, this is the confiding of the Spirit. God is Spirit....

Everything that earlier forms of piety (e.g., Luther) explained with the help of the devil, that it was the devil who sent sufferings, I explain with the help of God's majesty.

It cannot be otherwise if you really want God to be God and if you want to involve yourself with him. That is, if you are to be permitted to do the most blessed thing of all, to love God. Indeed, God can love the sparrow without that relationship becoming suffering, but in that case there cannot be any talk of a relationship of spirit or of loving God in return.[23]

Now we must return from Kierkegaard's radical vision to our partial parallel—and as we have now seen, the fundamental difference—between Kierkegaard and Thoreau. Here we must note that when it came to the relation to God, these two thinkers, so apparently similar in other ways, were radically different, even though both were alike in clinging stubbornly to their beliefs, right up to the point of death. Thoreau, dying, was asked by his aunt if he had made his peace with God, to which, reportedly, he replied blandly, "I was not aware that we had quarreled."[24] On the other hand, as he lay dying, Kierkegaard was asked by his best friend, who was a priest in the Danish State Church, if he wanted to take the sacrament. Kierkegaard, far more radical and otherworldly than Thoreau, replied polemically rather than blandly, "Yes, but not from a pastor, from a layman." And when his friend replied, "That would be quite difficult to arrange," Kierkegaard's rejoinder was, "Then I will die without it," explaining, "We cannot debate it. I have made my choice. I have chosen. The pastors are civil servants of the Crown and have nothing to do with Christianity."[25] Kierkegaard died without the sacrament, but it strains credulity to think that he died without the Christian faith. If any testimony to this is wanted, one need look no further than these discourses on *The Lily of the Field and the Bird of the Air.*

As part of his evolving understanding of the path and overall meaning of his development as a writer, Kierkegaard placed emphasis on the parallel-track architecture he saw running through the whole of his published work, in which an "aesthetic" work was "accompanied" by a "religious" one. Kierkegaard dated the start of his literary career from the publication of *Either/Or* in February 1843, and he viewed the appearance of that work as having been "concurrent" with the publication of *Two Edifying Discourses*, which, however, did not actually appear until May of that year.[26] *Either/Or* had been a great success and had sold out in less than two years. Now, in 1849, both in order to satisfy pent-up demand and as a much-needed source of income, Kierkegaard was publishing a second edition of *Either/Or*, and he took care to see that this aesthetic work was accompanied by the religious work, *The Lily of the Field and the Bird of the Air*. In a journal entry from May 1849, Kierkegaard wrote that these "three godly discourses ... accompany the second edition of *Either/Or* and mark the distinction between what is offered with the left hand and what is offered with the right."[27] I will return to the matter of offering a work with the "left" or "right" hand presently, but first will note that the works did indeed "accompany" one another. That is, in his timing of the release of the second edition of the aesthetic work *Either/Or* and the religious work *The Lily and the Bird*, Kierkegaard achieved his sought-after simultaneity much better than he had in connection with the first edition of *Either/Or*: this time, both the aesthetic work and the religious work were published on the same day, May 14, 1849. In the preface to *The Lily of the Field and the Bird of the Air*, Kierkegaard alludes specifically to this timing: "This little book (which with respect to the circumstances of its appearance reminds me of my first, and in particular of the first to my first, the preface to *Two Edifying Discourses* of 1843, which appeared immediately following *Either/Or*) will, I hope, bring the same recollection to … *my* reader." By "my first," Kierkegaard means his first collection of discourses, the *Two Edifying Discourses* of 1843, and by "the first to my first," he is referring to the preface to that collection, his first preface to his first collection of discourses, which he dated May 5, 1843, his thirtieth birthday, just as he dated the preface to the present volume May 5, 1849, his thirty-sixth birthday.

Furthermore, in his preface to *The Lily of the Field and the Bird of the Air*, Kierkegaard also expresses the hope that this preface "will remind [the reader], as it reminds me, of the preface to *Two Edifying Discourses* of 1844: 'It is offered with the right hand'—as opposed to the pseudonym, which was and is held out with the left." Here we come closer to understanding what Kierkegaard means by offering something with the "right" or "left" hand, and the way in which this is related to the matter of a "pseudonym." In order to understand what Kierkegaard is saying, his allusion, in the preface to the present work, to his preface to the *Two Edifying Discourses* of 1844, needs to be examined in a bit more detail. In the 1844 preface, Kierkegaard expressed the wish that his little book might "find what it seeks: that single individual whom I with joy and gratitude call *my* reader, who with the right hand receives what is offered with the right hand."[28] Kierkegaard deliberately uses this expression again in the preface to the present work, *The Lily and the Bird*, emphasizing that unlike the work of "the pseudonym, which was and is held out with the left," *these* discourses are offered with the *right* hand. In a journal entry from July 1849, Kierkegaard explains a bit more about what he means by this reference to "the pseudonym":

> Incidentally, it is quite remarkable that the preface to the three godly discourses about the lily and the bird came to have the wording "as opposed to the pseudonym, which was held out and is held out with the left." This is probably best understood in connection with the second printing of *Either/Or*, but it has also, of course, come to be significant with respect to the new pseudonym.[29]

Thus "the pseudonym" not only refers retrospectively to the pseudonymous authors of *Either/Or*, but also prospectively to "the new pseudonym," that is, to Anti-Climacus, the pseudonymous author of *The Sickness unto Death*—the work in which

Kierkegaard most clearly articulates his specifically Christian "anthropology," that is, his understanding of the human self as a self-relating relation that also has the capacity to relate itself to God—which, as noted, was published at the end of July 1849, just two and a half months after the publication of *The Lily of the Field and the Bird of the Air.*

Kierkegaard had first mentioned the notion of offering something with one's right hand in a journal entry from 1843: "Theodorus Atheos said that he offered his teachings with his right hand, but his listeners received them with their left hands."[30] Theodorus Atheos was the Epicurean philosopher Theodorus the Atheist of Cyrene (fourth century B.C.), who clearly intended his remark to be understood negatively, that is, that what he has offered with his right hand, his listeners accepted only with their left hands. Kierkegaard, however, changes the remark about *receiving* something with one's left hand into *giving* something with one's left hand, which apparently means that the giver remains at a remove, at secondhand, from what he or she gives, and that the recipient receives it in like fashion. And Kierkegaard links an author's *giving* with the *right* hand to a reader's *receiving* with the *right* hand, which presumably means that the giver relates firsthand to what he or she gives, so that the recipient also receives it firsthand and appropriates what is given. Thus it is significant that it is with his right hand that Kierkegaard offers us the discourses on *The Lily of the Field and the Bird of the Air.*

NOTES

1.   The text that forms the basis of the present translation of *Lilien paa Marken og Fuglen under Himlen. Tre gudelige Taler* is from the new, fifty-five-volume, Danish critical edition of all of Kierkegaard's writings: Niels Jørgen Cappelørn et al., eds., *Søren Kierkegaards Skrifter* [Søren Kierkegaard's Writings] (abbreviated hereafter as *SKS*) (Copenhagen: Gad, 1997–2012), vol. 11 (2006), pp. 5–48.

2.   For a full account of the genesis and publication of *The Lily of the Field and the Bird of the Air*, see Niels W. Bruun, Anne Mette Hansen, and Finn Gredal Jensen's "Critical Account of the Text" of *Lilien paa Marken og Fuglen under Himlen. Tre gudelige Taler* in *SKS*, vol. K11 (2006), pp. 7–33.

3. See entry NB4:154, in Bruce H. Kirmmse et al., eds. and trans., *Kierkegaard's Journals and Notebooks* (abbreviated hereafter as *KJN*), 11 vols. (Princeton, NJ: Princeton University Press, 2007– [vols. 1–8 published as of 2015]), vol. 4 (2011), pp. 357–358.

4. See Finn Gredal Jensen and Steen Tullberg's "Critical Account of the Text" of *Sygdommen til Døden* in *SKS*, vol. K11 (2006), pp. 156–167.

5. See Niels W. Bruun, Stine Holst Petersen, and Steen Tullberg's "Critical Account of the Text" of *Indøvelse i Christendommen* in *SKS*, vol. K12 (2008), pp. 66–93.

6. NB10:169, *KJN*, vol. 5 (2011), p. 352.

7. NB22:14, *KJN*, vol. 8 (2015), p. 109.

8. NB22:151, *KJN*, vol. 8, p. 184.

9. Ibid.

10. NB22:65, *KJN*, vol. 8, p. 136.

11. From Henry David Thoreau, *Walden*, first published in 1854, in Henry David Thoreau, *A Week on the Concord and Merrimack Rivers; Walden, or Life in the Woods; The Maine Woods; Cape Cod* (New York: Library of America, 1985), p. 329.

12. Henry David Thoreau, "Walking," in Henry David Thoreau, *Collected Essays and Poems* (New York: Library of America, 2001), p. 226.

13. Ibid.

14. DD:31, *KJN*, vol. 1 (2007), p. 223.

15. Søren Kierkegaard, *Kierkegaard: Letters and Documents*, trans. Henrik Rosenmeier (Princeton, NJ: Princeton University Press, 1978), p. 214.

16. Thoreau, *Walden*, p. 237.

17. NB12:49, *KJN*, vol. 6 (2012), p. 166.

18. Thoreau, *Walden*, p. 391.

19. DD:74, *KJN*, vol. 1, p. 276.

20. Søren Kierkegaard, *The Sickness unto Death*, trans. and ed. Howard V. Hong and Edna H. Hong (Princeton, NJ: Princeton University Press, 1980), p. 13.

21. Ibid., pp. 13–14.

22. NB25:58, *KJN*, vol. 8, p. 483.

23. NB27:39, *KJN*, vol. 9 (forthcoming, 2016); *SKS*, vol. 25 (2008), pp. 152–153.

24. Henry David Thoreau, *The Journal: 1837–1861*, ed. Damion Searls (New York: New York Review of Books, 2009), p. xxix.

25. Bruce H. Kirmmse, *Encounters with Kierkegaard* (Princeton, NJ: Princeton University Press, 1996), pp. 125–126.

26. In "The Accounting" Kierkegaard goes to great lengths to emphasize the simultaneity of *Either/Or* and the *Two Edifying Discourses* of 1843. See Søren Kierkegaard, *On My Work as an Author*, in *The Point of View*, trans. and ed. Howard V. Hong and Edna H. Hong (Princeton, NJ: Princeton University Press, 1999), pp. 5–11; see esp. p. 8.

27. NB11:53, *KJN*, vol. 6, p. 32.

28. See Søren Kierkegaard, *Eighteen Upbuilding Discourses,* trans. and ed. Howard V. Hong and Edna H. Hong (Princeton, NJ: Princeton University Press, 1990), p. 179.

29. NB12:10, *KJN*, vol. 6, p. 149 (translation slightly modified).

30. JJ:86, *KJN*, vol. 2 (2008), p. 154.

the lily of the field
and
the bird of the air

PREFACE

THIS LITTLE book (which with respect to the circumstances of its appearance reminds me of my first, and in particular of the first to my first, the preface to *Two Edifying Discourses* of 1843, which appeared immediately following *Either/Or*) will, I hope, bring the same recollection to "that single individual whom I with joy and gratitude call *my* reader": "It wishes to remain in concealment, just as it came into existence clandestinely—a little flower concealed in the great forest." The circumstances will remind the reader of this, and further, I hope, it will remind him, as it reminds me, of the preface to *Two Edifying Discourses* of 1844: "It is offered with the right hand"—as opposed to the pseudonym, which was and is held out with the left.

May 5th 1849.
S. K.

PRAYER

FATHER IN Heaven! That which we in the company of other people, especially in the throng of humanity, have such difficulty learning, and which, if we have learned it elsewhere, is so easily forgotten in the company of other people—what it is to be a human being and what, from a godly standpoint, is the requirement for being a human being—would that we might learn it, or, if it has been forgotten, that we might learn it anew from the lily and the bird; would that we might learn it, if not all at once, then learn at least something of it, little by little—would that on this occasion we might from the lily and the bird learn silence, obedience, joy!

No ONE can serve two masters, for he must either hate the one and love the other, or hold fast to one and despise the other. You cannot serve God and mammon. Therefore, I say to you, do not worry about your life, what you will eat and what you will drink, nor about your bodies, what you will wear. Is not life more than food and the body more than clothing? Look at the birds of the air; they neither sow, nor reap, nor gather into barns, and your heavenly Father feeds them. Are you not much more than they? But who among you can add one cubit to your height, even though you worry about it? And why do you worry about clothing? Consider the lilies of the field, how they grow; they neither toil nor spin. But I say to you that not even Solomon in all his splendor was arrayed like one of these. If God so clothes the grass of the field, which is today and is cast into the oven tomorrow, would he not much more clothe you, you of little faith! Therefore you should not worry, saying, "What shall we eat?" or "What shall we drink?" or "What shall we wear?"—the pagans seek all such things. For your heavenly Father knows that you need all these things. But seek first God's kingdom and his righteousness, and all these things will be added unto you. Therefore, do not worry about tomorrow, for tomorrow will worry about itself. Each day has troubles enough of its own. [Mt 6:24–34]

I

"LOOK AT THE BIRDS OF THE AIR; CONSIDER THE LILY OF THE FIELD."

BUT PERHAPS you say with "the poet" (and it very much appeals to you when the poet talks like this): "Oh, would that I were a bird, or would that I were like a bird, like the free bird, full of wanderlust, which flies far, far away over sea and land, so close to the sky, to far, faraway lands—alas for myself: I feel simply bound and yet again bound and nailed to the spot where daily worries and sufferings and difficulties make it clear to me that this is where I live—and for my whole life! Oh, would that I were a bird, or would that I were like a bird that, lighter than all earthly burdens, soars into the air, lighter than air—oh, would that I were like that light bird that, when it seeks a foothold, even builds its nest upon the

9

surface of the sea—alas for myself, for whom even the least movement—if I merely move—makes me feel what a burden rests upon me! Oh, would that I were a bird, or would that I were like a bird, free from all considerations, like the little songbird that humbly sings, even though no one listens to it—or that sings proudly, even though no one listens to it. Alas for myself: I have not a moment or anything for myself, but am parceled out and must serve thousands of considerations! Oh, would that I were a flower, or would that I were like the flower in the meadow, happily enamored of myself, period—alas for myself, who feel in my own heart that division of the human heart: neither to be capable of selfishly breaking with everything, nor capable of lovingly sacrificing everything!"

So much for "the poet." Listening superficially, it almost sounds as if he is saying what the gospel says—he indeed praises the happiness of the bird and the lily in the strongest terms. But now hear more. "Therefore, it is almost like cruelty for the gospel to praise the lily and the bird, saying: You shall be like them—alas for myself, I

10

in whom the wish is so true, so true, so true—
'Oh, would that I were like a bird of the air, like
a lily of the field.' But it is of course impossible
that I could become like them; that is precisely
why the wish is so fervent, so wistful, and yet so
burning in me. How cruel it is, then, for the gospel to speak like that to me; indeed, it is as if it
wanted to force me to lose my mind: that I *shall*
be what I feel altogether too deeply—just as deep
as the wish for it is within me—that I am not and
cannot be. I cannot understand the gospel; between us there is a difference of language that, if
I were to understand it, would kill me."

And that is how it always is with "the poet" in
relation to the gospel; for him it is the same with
respect to the gospel's words about being a child.
"Oh, would that I were a child," says the poet, or
"Would that I were like a child, 'Alas, a child,
innocent and happy'—alas, I have prematurely
become old and guilty and sorrowful!"

Strange, for of course, it is said quite rightly
that the poet is a child. And yet the poet cannot
come to an understanding with the gospel. For
the poet's life is really based upon despair of being

able to become what is wished for, and this despair begets the wish. But "the wish" is the invention of disconsolateness. For of course the wish
provides momentary consolation, but upon closer
inspection it can be seen that it does not in fact
console. And therefore we say that the wish is
the consolation that disconsolateness invents. Re-
markable self-contradiction! Yes, but the poet is
also this self-contradiction. The poet is the child
of pain, whom the father nonetheless calls the
son of joy. In the poet, the wish came into existence in pain; and this wish, this burning wish,
gives joy to the human heart more than wine de-
lights it, more than the earliest bud of spring,
more than the first star that a person, weary of
the day, greets in longing for the night, more than
the last star in the sky to which a person bids
farewell when day dawns. The poet is the child
of eternity but lacks the earnestness of eternity.
When he thinks of the lily and the bird, he weeps;
as he weeps, he finds relief in weeping; "the wish"
comes into existence, along with the eloquence of
the wish: "Oh, would that I were a bird, the bird
of whom I read in the picture book when I was a

child; oh, would that I were a flower in the field, the flower that stood in my mother's garden." But if, with the gospel, one were to say to him, "This is in earnest, precisely this is the earnestness, that the bird is the teacher in earnest," the poet would have to laugh—and he makes a joke of the bird and the lily, so wittily that he gets us all to laugh, even the most earnest person who has ever lived; but he does not move the gospel in the same way. The gospel is so earnest that all the poet's sadness fails to change it even though it changes the most earnest person, so that for a moment he yields, goes along with the poet's thoughts, sighs with him and says, "Dear fellow, it really is an impossibility for you. Well then, I dare not say 'You shall.'" But the gospel *does* dare command the poet that he *shall* be like the bird. And so earnest is the gospel that the poet's most irresistible invention does not cause it to smile.

You "shall" become a child again, and therefore, or to that end, you shall begin by being able to and by willing to understand the words that are as if directed at a child, and which every child understands—you shall understand the words as a child understands them: "You *shall*." The child never asks about reasons; the child does not dare do so, neither does the child need to—and the one corresponds to the other, for precisely because the child does not dare do so, neither does it need to ask about reasons; because for the child it is reason enough that it shall—indeed, all reasons together would not be reason enough to the child to the degree that this is. And the child never says, "I cannot." The child does not dare do so, and neither is it true—the one corresponds precisely to the other—for precisely because the child does not dare say, "I cannot," it is not therefore true that it cannot, and it therefore turns out that the truth is that it can do it, for it is impossible to be unable to do it when one does not dare do otherwise: nothing is more certain—as long as it is certain that one does not dare do otherwise. And the child never looks for an evasion or an excuse, for the child understands the frightful truth that there is no evasion or excuse, there is no hiding place, neither in heaven nor on earth, neither in the parlor nor in the garden, where it could hide from this "You shall." And when it is

14

quite certain to a person that there is no such hiding place, then neither is there any evasion or excuse. And when one knows the frightful truth that there is no evasion or excuse—well, then one naturally refrains from finding it, for what *is* not cannot be found—but one also refrains from seeking it; and then one does what one shall. And the child never needs to spend a long time in deliberation, for when it shall—and perhaps immediately— then there is no occasion for deliberation; and even were this not the case, when, after all, it *shall*: Yes, even if one were to give it an eternity to deliberate, the child would not need it; the child would say, "Why all this time, when, after all, I shall?" And if the child were to take the time, it would surely use the time in another manner, for play, for enjoyment, and the like—for what the child shall, the child shall; that is unalterable and has absolutely nothing to do with deliberation.

Therefore, in accordance with the instructions of the gospel, let us in earnest regard the lily and the bird as teachers. In earnest, for the gospel is not so intellectually pretentious as to be unable to make use of the lily and the bird; but neither is it so worldly that it is only capable of regarding the lily and the bird mournfully or with a smile.

From the lily and the bird as teachers, let us learn

silence, or learn to **keep silent.**

For surely it is speech that places the human being above the animal, and if you like, far above the lily. But because the ability to speak is an advantage, it does not follow that there is no art in the ability to keep silent, or that it would be an inferior art. On the contrary, precisely because a human being has the ability to speak, for this very reason the ability to keep silent is an art; and precisely because this advantage of his tempts him so easily, the ability to keep silent is a great art. But this he can learn from the silent teachers, the lily and the bird.

"Seek first God's kingdom and his righteousness."

But what does it mean, what is it that I must do, what sort of effort is it of which it can be said that

it seeks, that it aspires to, God's kingdom? Shall
I seek to secure a position that corresponds to my
abilities and strengths, so that I can be effective
in it? No, you shall *first* seek God's kingdom.
Shall I give all my fortune to the poor, then? No,
first you shall seek God's kingdom. Shall I go out
and proclaim this teaching to the world, then?
No, you shall *first* seek God's kingdom. But then,
in a certain sense is there in fact nothing I shall
do? Yes, quite true, in a certain sense there is
nothing. You shall in the deepest sense make
yourself nothing, become nothing before God,
learn to keep silent. In this silence is the beginning, which is *first* to seek God's kingdom.

Thus, in a godly way, does one come in a certain sense backward to the beginning. The beginning is not that with which one begins but is that
to which one comes, and one comes to it backward. Beginning is this art of *becoming* silent, for
there is no art in keeping silent as nature is. And
in the deepest sense, this becoming silent, silent
before God, is the beginning of the fear of God,
for as the fear of God is the beginning of wisdom,
so is silence the beginning of the fear of God.

17

And as the fear of God is more than the beginning of wisdom, *is* "wisdom," so is silence more than the beginning of the fear of God, *is* "the fear of God." In this silence, the many thoughts of wishing and desiring fall silent in the fear of God; in this silence, the loquacity of thanksgiving falls silent in the fear of God.

The ability to speak is the human being's superiority over the animal, but in relation to God wanting to speak can easily become corrupting for the human being, who is able to speak. God is in heaven, the human being is on earth: therefore they cannot very well talk with one another. God is infinite wisdom, what the human being knows is idle chatter: therefore they cannot very well talk with one another. God is love; the human being is—as one says to a child—even a little fool with respect to his or her own well-being: therefore they cannot very well talk with one another. Only in much fear and trembling can a human being talk with God, in much fear and trembling. But to speak in much fear and trembling is difficult for another reason, for as anxiety causes the voice to falter in a physical sense, so also does great fear and trembling surely cause the voice to fall mute in silence. This is known by the person who prays rightly, and this is perhaps exactly what the person who did not pray rightly has learned in prayer. There was something that was very much on his mind, a matter that was so important for him to have God understand properly; he was afraid that he might have forgotten something in his prayer—alas, and if he had forgotten it, he was afraid that God would not have remembered it on his own: therefore, he wanted to gather his thoughts and pray truly fervently. And then, if he in fact prayed truly fervently, what happened to him? Something strange and wonderful happened to him: gradually, as he became more and more fervent in prayer, he had less and less to say, and finally he became entirely silent. He became silent. Indeed, he became what is, if possible, even more the opposite of talking than silence: he became a listener. He had thought that to pray was to talk; he learned that to pray is not only to keep silent, but to listen. And that is how it is: to pray is not to listen to oneself speak, but is to come to keep silent, and to continue

19

keeping silent, to wait, until the person who prays hears God.

That is why, in serving as one's upbringing, the words of the gospel, "Seek *first* God's kingdom," muzzle a person's mouth, as it were, by answering every question he poses—about whether *this* is what he shall do—with "No, you shall *first* seek God's kingdom." And this is why one can paraphrase the gospel's words as follows: "You shall begin by praying, not as though—as we have of course shown—prayer always begins with silence, but because when prayer has properly become prayer, it has become silence. Seek first God's kingdom, that is: Pray!" If you were to ask—indeed, if in your questioning you went through every individual thing, asking: "Is it this that I shall do, and if I do it, is this, then, seeking God's kingdom?"—the answer must be: "No, you shall first seek God's kingdom." But to pray, that is, to pray rightly, is to become silent, and that is to seek first God's kingdom.

You can learn this silence from the lily and the bird. That is, their silence is no art, but when *you* become silent like the lily and the bird, then you are at the beginning, which is *first* to seek God's kingdom.

How solemn it is out there under God's heaven with the lily and the bird—and why? Ask "the poet." He replies, "Because there is silence." And he longs to be out in that solemn silence, away from the worldliness of the human world, where there is so much talk—away from all the worldly life of humanity, which merely demonstrates in a sorry way that it is speech that distinguishes human beings from animals. "Because," the poet would say, "if that is really a way in which to distinguish oneself—no, then I find the silence out there very, very much preferable. I prefer it—no, there is no comparison—it distinguishes itself as infinitely above human beings, who are capable of speech." For the poet thinks he perceives the voice of God in the silence of nature. Not only does he not think that he perceives the voice of God in the busy talk of human beings, he does not even think that he can perceive that humanity has kinship with divinity. The poet says, "Speech is the human being's advantage over the animal, to be sure—if he is able to *keep silent*."

But the ability to keep silent is something you can learn out there in the company of the lily and the bird, where there is silence and also something of divinity in that silence. There is silence out there, and not only when everything keeps silent in the silence of night, but also when a thousand strings are in motion all day long and everything is a sea of sound, as it were—and nonetheless there is silence out there: each one in particular does it so well that not one of them, and none of them all together, do anything to break the solemn silence. There is silence out there. The forest keeps silent; even when it whispers, it is nonetheless silent. For the trees, even where they stand most closely together, keep their word to one another—which human beings do so infrequently, despite having given their word that "This will remain between us." The sea keeps silent; even when it rages loudly, it is nonetheless silent. At first, you perhaps hear incorrectly, and you hear it rage. If you rush away bearing that message, you do the sea an injustice. On the other hand, if you take your time and listen more carefully, you will hear—how amazing!—you will hear the silence, for uniformity is of course also silence. When the silence of evening descends upon the countryside, and you hear the distant lowing of cattle from the meadow, or you hear the familiar voice of the dog from the farmer's house, it cannot be said that this lowing or the dog's voice disturbs the silence—no, this is a part of the silence, it has a secret, and thus a silent, understanding with the silence; it increases it.

Let us now look more closely at the lily and the bird from whom we are to learn. The bird *keeps silent and waits*: it knows, or rather it fully and firmly believes, that everything takes place at its appointed time. Therefore the bird waits, but it knows that it is not granted to it to know the hour or the day; therefore it keeps silent. "It will surely take place at the appointed time," the bird says. Or no, the bird does not say this, but keeps silent. But its silence speaks, and its silence says that it believes it, and because it believes it, it keeps silent and waits. Then, when the moment comes, the silent bird understands that this is the moment; it makes use of it and is never put to shame. This is also how it is with the lily, it keeps silent and waits. It does not ask impatiently, "When is the spring coming?" because it knows that it will come at the appointed time; it knows that it would not benefit in any way whatever if it were permitted to determine the seasons of the year. It does not say, "When will we get rain?" or "When will we have sunshine?" or "Now we have had too much rain," or "Now it is too hot." It does not ask in advance how the summer will be this year, how long or short; no, it keeps silent and waits—that is how simple it is, but nonetheless it is never deceived, something that of course can only happen to shrewdness, not to simplicity, which does not deceive and is not deceived. Then the moment comes, and when the moment comes, the silent lily understands that now is the moment, and makes use of it. Oh, you profound teachers of simplicity, should it not also be possible to encounter "the moment" when one is speaking? No. Only by keeping silent does one encounter the moment. When one speaks, even if one says only a single word, one misses the moment. Only in silence *is* the moment. And this is surely why it so rarely happens that a human being properly comes to understand when the moment is and how to make proper use of the moment—because he cannot keep silent. He cannot keep silent and wait; this perhaps explains why the moment never comes for him at all. He cannot keep silent; this perhaps explains why he did not notice the moment when it came for him. Even though it is pregnant with rich significance, the moment does not send forth any herald in advance to announce its arrival; it comes too swiftly for that; indeed, there is not a moment's time beforehand. Nor, no matter how significant it is in itself, does the moment come with commotion or shouting; no, it comes softly, on lighter feet than the lightest tread of any creature, for it comes with the light step of the sudden; it comes stealthily. Therefore one must be utterly silent if one is to perceive that "now it is here." And at the next moment it is gone. Therefore one must be utterly silent if one is to succeed in making use of it. But of course everything depends upon "the moment." And this is surely the misfortune in the lives of many, of far the greater part of humanity: that they never perceived "the moment," that in their lives the eternal and the temporal were exclusively separated. And why? Because they could not keep silent.

The bird *keeps silent and suffers*. However much heartache it has, it keeps silent. Even the melancholic mourning dove of the desert or of solitude keeps silent. It sighs three times and then keeps silent, sighs again three times, but is essentially silent. For what it is it does not say; it does not complain; it accuses no one; it sighs only to fall silent again. Indeed, it is as if the silence would cause it to burst; therefore it must sigh in order to keep silent. The bird is not free of suffering, but the silent bird frees itself from what makes the suffering more burdensome: from the misunderstood sympathy of others; frees itself from what makes the suffering last longer: from all the talk of suffering; frees itself from what makes the suffering into something worse than suffering: from the sin of impatience and sadness. Do not think that the bird is just being a bit duplicitous by keeping silent when it suffers; do not think that, however silent it is in relation to others, the bird is not in fact silent in its innermost being, that it complains over its fate, accuses God and human beings, and lets its "heart in sorrow sin." No, the bird keeps silent and suffers. Alas, the human being does not do this. But why is it, indeed, that human suffering, compared with that of the bird, seems so frightful? Is it not because the human being can speak? No, not because of that, for that is of course an advantage, but because a human being cannot keep silent. No, the situation is not as the impatient person—and even more emphatically, the despairing person—believes he understands it to be, when he (and this itself is a misuse of speech and of the voice) when he says or cries: "Would that I had a voice like that of the storm, that I could express all my suffering as I feel it!" Ah, that would be but a poor remedy; to the degree he did this, he would only feel his suffering all the more strongly. No, but if you could keep silent, if you had the silence of the bird, the suffering would surely become less.

And as with the bird, so with the lily: it keeps silent. Even though it stands and suffers while it withers, it keeps silent. The innocent child cannot dissemble—nor is it required that it do so, and it is the child's good fortune that it cannot, for truly, the art of dissembling is purchased dearly. It cannot dissemble and can do nothing about the fact that its color changes and that it thereby betrays something we of course know from this pallid change of color: that it is suffering; but it remains silent. It would like to stand erect in order to conceal what it suffers, but it lacks the strength, the self-mastery, for this: its head nods, exhausted and bent; the passerby—if, in fact, any passerby has sympathy enough to notice it!—the passerby understands what this means, it is eloquent enough. But the lily keeps silent. This is how it is with the lily. But how is it that human suffering, compared with that of the lily, seems so frightful? Is it not because the human being can speak? If the lily could speak, and if—alas, like the human being—it had not learned the art of keeping silent, would not its suffering also become frightful? But the lily keeps silent. For the lily, to suffer is to suffer, neither more nor less. But precisely when to suffer is neither more nor less than to suffer, the suffering is narrowed and simplified and diminished as much as possible. The suffering cannot become less, for of course it *is*, and thus it is what it is. But on the other hand, the suffering can become infinitely greater when it does not remain exactly what it is, neither more nor less. When the suffering does not become greater or less, that is, when the suffering is only the definite thing it is, even if it were the greatest suffering, it is the least it can be. But when it becomes indefinite how great the suffering is, the suffering becomes greater; this indefiniteness increases the suffering infinitely. And this indefiniteness emerges precisely because of the human being's dubious advantage of being able to speak. On the other hand, the definiteness of suffering— the fact that it is neither more nor less than it is—is attained only by being able to keep silent, and you can learn this silence from the bird and the lily.

Out there with the bird and the lily there is silence. But what does this silence express? It expresses respect for God, for the fact that it is he who rules and he alone to whom wisdom and understanding belong. And just because this silence is respect for God, is worship—as it can be in nature—this silence is so solemn. And because this silence is solemn in this way, a person perceives God in nature—so what wonder is it, indeed, that everything keeps silent out of respect for him! Even if *he* does not speak, the fact that everything keeps silent out of respect for him of course affects one as if he spoke.

What you can learn, however, from the silence out there with the lily and the bird without the help of any "poet," what only the gospel can teach you, is that it is earnestness, that it shall be earnestness, that the lily and the bird *shall* be the teachers, that you shall imitate them, learn from them in all earnestness, that you shall become silent as the lily and the bird.

And indeed, this is already earnestness—when it is properly understood, not as by the dreaming poet or by the poet who lets nature dream of him—this: that out there with the lily and the bird you perceive that *you are before God*, which most often is quite entirely forgotten in talking and conversing with other people. For when just two of us talk together, even more so when we are ten or more, it is so easily forgotten that you and

30

I, that we two, or that we ten, are before God. But the lily, who is the teacher, is profound. It does not involve itself with you at all; it keeps silent, and by keeping silent it wants to signify to you that you are before God, so that you remember that you are before God—so that you also might earnestly and in truth become silent before God.

And you *shall* become silent before God like the lily and the bird. You shall not say, "The lily and the bird, of course they can keep silent; after all, they cannot speak." You must not say this; you must say nothing whatever; you must not make the least attempt to render instruction in silence impossible—instead of keeping silent in earnest—by foolishly and meaninglessly jumbling silence together with speaking, perhaps as the subject of speaking, so that nothing comes of the silence, but instead a speech comes into existence, a speech about keeping silent. Before God, you shall not become more important to yourself than a lily or a bird—but when it becomes earnestness and truth that you are before God, the latter will follow from the former. And even if what you want to accomplish in the world were the most amazing feat: you shall acknowledge the lily and the bird as your teachers and before God you are not to become more important to yourself than the lily and the bird. And even if the entire world were not large enough to contain all your plans when you unfold them, with the lily and the bird as teachers, you shall learn before God to be able simply to fold all your plans together into something that occupies less space than a point, and makes less noise than the most insignificant trifle: in silence. And even if what you suffered in the world were as agonizing as anything ever experienced, you shall acknowledge the lily and the bird as your teachers and not become more important to yourself than the lily and the bird are to themselves in their little cares.

This is how it is when the gospel means in earnest that the bird and the lily shall be the teachers. It is otherwise with the poet or with the person who—precisely because earnestness is lacking—does not become utterly silent in the presence of the lily and the bird, but becomes a poet. True enough, the speech of the poet is very different from ordinary human speech, so solemn that in comparison with ordinary speech it is almost like silence, but it is not in fact silence. Nor does "the poet" seek silence in order to become silent, but the reverse, in order to speak—as a poet speaks. Out there in the silence the poet dreams of the exploit—which, however, he will not carry out, because the poet is of course not a hero. And he becomes eloquent—perhaps he becomes eloquent precisely because he is the unhappy lover of the exploit, whereas the hero is its happy lover. Thus, because the privation makes him eloquent, as privation essentially makes the poet, he becomes eloquent: this, his eloquence, is the poem. Out there in the silence he sketches great plans for reshaping the whole world and making it happy, great plans that are never realized—no, they of course become the poem. Out there in the silence he broods over his pain, makes everything—indeed, even the teachers, the lily and the bird, must serve him instead of teaching him—he makes everything echo his pain, and this echo of pain is the poem, for a cry pure and simple is no poem, but the infinite echo of the cry in itself is the poem.

Thus the poet does not become silent in the silence of the lily and the bird, and why not? Simply because he reverses the relationship and makes himself into something more important in comparison with the lily and bird, even imagining that he is meritorious for having, as is said, lent words and speech to the bird and the lily—whereas the task was that he himself learn silence from the lily and the bird.

Oh, but would that the gospel might succeed, with the help of the lily and the bird, in teaching you, my listener, earnestness, and in teaching me to make you utterly silent before God! Would that in the silence you might forget yourself, forget what you yourself are called, your own name, the famous name, the lowly name, the insignificant name, in order in silence to pray to God, "Hallowed be *your* name!" Would that in silence you might forget yourself, your plans, the great, all-encompassing plans, or the limited plans concerning your life and its future, in order in silence to pray to God, "Your kingdom come!" Would that you might in silence forget your will, your willfulness, in order in silence to pray to God,

"*Your* will be done!" Yes, if you could learn from the lily and the bird to become utterly silent before God, what, then, wouldn't the gospel be able to help you do—then nothing would be impossible for you. But if the gospel, with the help of the lily and the bird, has merely taught you silence, how much has it not helped you already! For as the fear of God, as is said, is the beginning of wisdom, so is silence the beginning of the fear of God. Go to the ant and become wise, says Solomon; go to the bird and the lily and learn silence, says the gospel.

"Seek *first* God's kingdom and his righteousness." But the expression of the fact that one is seeking first God's kingdom is precisely silence, the silence of the lily and the bird. The lily and the bird seek God's kingdom and absolutely nothing else; all the rest will be added unto them. But then, are they not seeking God's kingdom first if they seek nothing else whatever? How is it, then, that the gospel says: Seek *first* God's kingdom, thereby implying that in its view there is something else to be sought next, regardless of the fact that it is indeed clear that the gospel's view is that God's kingdom is the only thing that is to be sought? This is surely because it is undeniable that God's kingdom can only be sought when it is sought first; the person who does not seek God's kingdom first does not seek it at all. Furthermore, this is because the ability to seek includes in itself a possibility of being able to seek something else, and therefore the gospel—which of course for the time being is external to a person, who is thus capable of seeking something else—says, "You shall first seek God's kingdom." And finally, it is because the gospel gently and lovingly condescends to the human being, persuading him bit by bit in order to entice him to the good. Were the gospel immediately to say, "You shall simply and solely seek God's kingdom," it would surely seem that too much was required of a person. Half in impatience, half in fear and anxiety, he would shrink back. But now the gospel accommodates itself to him a little. There stands the human being, viewing the many things he wants to seek—then the gospel addresses him and says, "Seek first God's kingdom." Then the human being thinks, "Well, then, if afterward I am permitted to seek other things, let me begin by seeking God's kingdom." If he then actually begins by doing this, the gospel knows well what will come next, that he will in fact be so satisfied and sated by this search that he will simply forget to seek anything else—indeed, that there is nothing he wants to do less than seek something else—so that it now becomes true that he simply and solely seeks God's kingdom. That is how the gospel goes about it, and of course this is how an adult speaks to a child. Imagine a child who is truly hungry; when the mother places food on the table and the child gets to see what is there, it is almost ready to cry with impatience and says: "What good will that little bit do? When I have eaten it, I will be just as hungry." Perhaps the child even becomes so impatient that it simply refuses to start eating, "because that little bit cannot do any good." But the mother, who knows well that it is all a misunderstanding, says: "Yes, yes, my little friend, just eat this first, then we can always see about getting a little more." Then the child begins, and what happens? The child is full before half of it is eaten. Had the mother immediately reprimanded the child and said, "That is indeed more than enough," the mother would of course not have been wrong, but her conduct would not have exemplified the wisdom appropriate to upbringing, as it now in fact did. This is how it is with the gospel. The most important thing for the gospel is not to reprimand and scold; what is most important for the gospel is to get human beings to follow its guidance. That is why it says, "Seek first." In so doing, it muzzles, so to speak, all of a person's objections, brings him to silence, and gets him actually to begin first this seeking. And then this seeking satisfies a human being in such a way that it now becomes true that he simply and solely seeks God's kingdom.

Seek first God's kingdom; that is, become like the lily and the bird; that is, become utterly silent before God: then all the rest will be added unto you.

II

"NO ONE CAN SERVE TWO
MASTERS, FOR HE MUST
EITHER HATE THE ONE
AND LOVE THE OTHER, OR
HOLD FAST TO ONE AND
DESPISE THE OTHER."

My LISTENER! You know that there is often talk of an either/or in the world; and this either/or gives rise to a great commotion, involving various sorts of people in the most various ways, in hope, in fear, in busy activity, in tense inactivity, etc. You also know that in this same world people have heard it said that no either/or exists, and that this wisdom has given rise to just as much commotion as has the most significant either/or. But out here in the silence with the lily and the bird, should it be doubtful here that an either/or exists? Or should it be doubtful here what this either/or is? Or should it be doubtful here whether this either/or is in the deepest sense the only either/or?

No, here, in this solemn silence, not only under God's heaven, but in this solemn silence before God—here there can be no doubt about it. There is an either/or: either *God*—or, well, then the rest is a matter of indifference; whatever else a human being chooses, if he does not choose God he misses either/or, or he is in perdition through his either/or. Thus: either *God*—you see, there is no emphasis whatever placed on the alternative except by contrast to God, whereby the emphasis falls infinitely upon God. So it is actually God who, by being himself the object of the choice, tightens the decision of the choice into truly becoming an either/or. If a human being were capable of thinking, in frivolous or melancholic fashion, that where God is present as the One, there were actually three things to choose among—he is lost, or he has lost God, and therefore there is actually no either/or for him. For with God, when the notion of God disappears or is distorted, the either/or also disappears. But how could this happen to anyone in the silence with the lily and the bird!

Thus: either/or. Either God, and as the gospel explains it, either love God *or* hate him. Yes, when you are surrounded by commotion or when you are immersed in diversions, this seems to be almost an exaggeration; there seems to be altogether too great a distance between loving and hating to permit someone to place them so close to one another, in a single breath, in a single thought, in two words that—without subordinate clauses, without parenthetical phrases to produce greater agreement, without even the slightest punctuation mark—follow immediately upon one another. But indeed, as a body falls with infinite speed when placed in a vacuum, so also does the silence out there with the lily and the bird, the solemn silence before God, cause these two opposites to touch and repel one another at exactly the same instant: indeed, they come into existence in the same instant—either to love or to hate. No more than the airless vacuum constitutes a third factor that delays a falling body, does this solemn silence before God constitute a third

factor that could keep loving and hating at a de-
laying distance from each other.—Either God,
and as the gospel explains it, either hold fast to
God *or* despise him. In human society, in everyday dealings, in associating with the multitude,
there seems to be a great distance between hold-
ing fast to someone and despising him: "I do not
need to associate with that person," someone says,
"but of course it by no means follows from this
that I despise him, not at all." And this is indeed
how it is in relation to the many people with
whom a person associates in social talkativeness
and without essential inwardness, more or less in-
differently. But the smaller the number becomes,
the less talkative social intercourse becomes—that
is, the more inward it becomes—the more does
an either/or begin to become the law for the relationship. And intercourse with God is in the
deepest sense unsociable, unconditionally so. Just
take two lovers, a relationship that is also unsociable, precisely because it is so inward: the rule
for them and their relationship is: either we hold
fast to one another or we despise one another.
And now, in the silence before God with the lily

and the bird, where absolutely no one else is present, thus where there is absolutely no other asso-
ciation for you than with God—yes, then the rule
is: either hold fast to him or despise him. There is
no excuse, because no one else is present, and in
any case there is no one else present in such a way
that you can hold fast to him without despising
God, for precisely in this silence it is clear how
close God is to you. The two lovers are so close to
one another that as long as the other is alive the
one cannot hold fast to another without *despising*
the other; therein lies the either/or of this relationship. Whether this either/or (either hold fast—or
despise) exists depends on how close the two are
to one another. But God, who of course never
dies, is even closer to you, infinitely closer, than
two lovers are to one another—he, your Creator
and Sustainer; he, in whom you live, move, and
have your being; he, by the grace of whom you
have everything. So it is no exaggeration, this either to hold fast to God or to despise him; it is not
as when a person proposes an either/or in connection with something insignificant, a person of
whom one thus may properly say, "He is brusque."

That is not how things are here. For, on the one hand, God, of course, is surely God. And on the other hand, he does not set forth an either/or in relation to something insignificant; he does not say, "Either a rose or a tulip," but he sets it forth in relation to himself and says: "Either *me* ... either you hold fast to me unconditionally in everything, or you—despise me." Yet God certainly could not speak otherwise of himself. If God should—or could—speak of himself as though he were not absolutely number 1, as though he were not the only one, unconditionally everything, but merely sort of a something, someone who had hopes of perhaps being included in our consideration—then God must of course have lost himself, lost the notion of himself, and would not be God.

Thus in the silence with the lily and the bird there is an either/or, either God ... and understood as follows: either love him or—hate him, either hold fast to him or—despise him.

Then what does this either/or mean, what does God require? For either/or is a requirement, just as the lovers of course require love when the

44

one says to the other, "Either/or." But God does not relate to you as a lover, nor do you relate to him as a lover. The relationship is different: it is that of the creature to the Creator. What, then, does he require with this either/or? He requires obedience, unconditional obedience; if you are not obedient in everything, unconditionally, then you do not love him, and if you do not love him, then—you hate him. If you are not obedient in everything unconditionally, then you do not hold fast to him. Or, if you do not hold fast to him unconditionally and in everything, you do not hold fast to him; and if you do not hold fast to him, then—you despise him.

This unconditional obedience—that if one does not love God, one hates him, that if one does not hold fast to him unconditionally and in everything, one despises him—this unconditional obedience you can learn from the teachers to which the gospel refers, the lily and the bird. It is said that in learning to obey one learns to rule, but what is even more certain is that by being obedient oneself one can teach obedience. So it is with the lily and the bird. They have no power with which to compel the learner, they have only the compulsion of their own obedience. The lily and the bird are "the obedient teachers." Is this not a strange way of speaking? In other cases, "obedient" is of course the word one uses of the learner; it is required of him that he be obedient; but here it is the teacher himself who is obedient! And in what does he give instruction? In obedience. And how does he give instruction? By obedience. If you were able to be obedient in the same way as the lily and the bird, you would also be able to teach obedience by obedience. But since neither you nor I are obedient in that way, let us from the lily and the bird learn:

obedience.

Out there with the lily and the bird there is silence, we said. But this silence—or what we strove to learn from it, to become silent—is the first condition for truly being able to obey. When everything around you is solemn silence, as it is out there, and when there is silence within you, then you perceive—and you perceive it with the emphasis of the infinite—the truth of this: You shall love the Lord your God and serve him alone. And you perceive that it is "you," you who shall love God in this way, you alone in the whole world, you who are indeed alone, surrounded by the solemn silence: alone in such a way that every doubt, every objection, every excuse, every evasion, and every question—in short, every voice— is reduced to silence within you: every voice, that is, every voice other than that of God, which around you and within you speaks to you through the silence. Were there never silence around you and within you in this way, then you would never have learned and never will learn obedience. But if you have learned silence, then it will surely be possible to learn obedience.

Pay attention, then, to nature, which surrounds you. In nature everything is obedience, unconditional obedience. Here "God's will is done, as in heaven, so also on earth." Or if one were to cite the holy words in another way, they would still be fitting: here in nature "God's will is done on earth as it is in heaven." In nature everything is unconditional obedience; here it is not merely the case that (as is also true in the world of human beings) inasmuch as God is the Almighty, nothing, not the least thing, happens without it being his will—no, here it is also because everything is unconditional obedience. But this, after all, is certainly an infinite difference: for it is one thing that the most cowardly and most defiant human disobedience cannot—that the disobedience of an individual human being or of the entire human race cannot—do the least thing against his will, he the Almighty; it is something else that his will is done because everything obeys him unconditionally, because there is no other will than his in heaven and on earth; and this is the case in nature. In nature it is the case that, as scripture says, "not one sparrow falls to the ground without his will." And this is so not only because he is the Almighty, but because everything is unconditional obedience; his will is the only thing: there is not the least objection; not a word, not a sigh is heard; the unconditionally obedient sparrow falls to the ground in unconditional obedience if it is God's will. In nature, everything is unconditional obedience. The sighing of the wind, the echo of the forest, the murmuring of the brook, the hum of summer, the whispering of the leaves, the hiss of the grass, every sound, every sound you hear, it is all compliance, unconditional obedience, so that in it you can hear God as you can hear him in the music of the obedient movement of the heavenly bodies. And the impetuous turbulence of wind, the light pliability of the clouds, the dripping fluidity and cohesiveness of the sea, the speed of a ray of light, and the even greater speed of sound: all this is obedience. And the rise of the sun at a given hour, and its setting at a given hour, and the shift of the wind at God's command, and the rise and fall of the tides at set times, and the agreement of the seasons of the year in their precise alternation: everything, everything, everything is obedience. Yes, were there a star in the heavens that wanted to have its own will, or a speck of dust on earth: they are instantly annihilated, and with equal ease. For in nature everything is nothing, understood in the sense that there is nothing other than God's unconditional will; at the same instant that it is not unconditionally God's will, it has ceased to exist.

Let us, then, observe the lily and bird more closely, and from a human perspective, in order to learn obedience. The lily and the bird are unconditionally obedient to God. They are masters at this. As befits teachers, they have a masterful understanding of how to encounter the unconditioned—something that, alas, most people surely miss and at which they fail. For there is one thing that the lily and bird unconditionally do not understand, that, alas, most people understand best: half-measures. That a minor bit of disobedience would not be unconditional disobedience is something the lily and the bird cannot and do not want to understand. That the least little bit of disobedience would truly have any name other than contempt for God is something the lily and the bird cannot and do not want to understand. That there should be anything else or anyone else that a person, being divided, could *also* serve in addition to serving God, and that this would not also be despising God: this is something that the bird

50

NO ONE CAN SERVE TWO MASTERS

and the lily cannot and do not want to understand.
Marvelous security in encountering the unconditioned and having one's life in it! And yet, o you
profound teachers, could it really be possible to
find security anywhere else than in the unconditioned, since in itself the conditioned is of course
insecurity! Then I would certainly rather speak
differently; I would not admire the security with
which they encounter the unconditioned, but
would rather say that it is precisely the unconditioned that gives them the admirable security
that makes them teachers of obedience. For the
lily and the bird are unconditionally obedient to
God; in their obedience they are so simple or so
lofty *that they believe that everything that happens
is unconditionally God's will, and that they have absolutely nothing to do in the world other than either to
carry out God's will in unconditional obedience or to
submit to God's will in unconditional obedience.*

If the place assigned to the lily is really as unfortunate as possible, so that it can be easily foreseen
that it will be totally superfluous all its life, not be

noticed by a single person who might find joy in it; if the place and the surroundings are—yes, I had forgotten it was the lily of which we are speaking—are so "desperately" unfortunate, that not only is it not visited, but is avoided: the obedient lily obediently submits to its circumstances and bursts forth in all its loveliness. We human beings—or rather, a human being in the lily's situation—would say: "It is hard, it is unendurable, when one is a lily and is as lovely as a lily, then to be assigned a place in such a location, to have to bloom there, in surroundings that are as unfavorable as possible, that are as if calculated to annihilate the impression of one's loveliness. No, it is unendurable. It is of course a self-contradiction on the part of the Creator!" That is how a human being, or we human beings, would certainly think and speak if we were in the lily's place, and then we would wither from grief. But the lily thinks differently, it thinks as follows: "Of course, I myself cannot determine the location and the circumstances; this is thus not my affair in the least way; that I stand where I stand is God's will." That is how the lily thinks. And that things actually are as it thinks—that this is God's will—can be seen from its appearance, for it is lovely: Solomon in all his splendor was not arrayed like this. Ah, if one lily differed from another in its loveliness, this lily would have to be awarded the prize: it possesses one additional loveliness, for there is really no art to being lovely when one is a lily, but to be lovely in these circumstances and in such surroundings, which do everything they can to hinder it—fully to be oneself in such surroundings, and to preserve oneself, to mock all the power of the surroundings—no, not to mock, lilies do not do that, but to be entirely carefree in all one's loveliness! For despite its surroundings the lily is itself because it is unconditionally obedient to God; and because it is unconditionally obedient to God, it is unconditionally free of cares, which only those who are unconditionally obedient—especially under such circumstances—can be. And because it is wholly and fully itself and is unconditionally free of cares—two things that correspond to one another directly and inversely—it is lovely. Only through unconditional obedience can one unconditionally encounter "the place"

53

where one is to stand; and when one encounters it unconditionally, then one understands that it is unconditionally a matter of indifference even if "the place" is a dunghill.—Even if the situation that the lily encounters at precisely the moment it is to spring forth is as unfortunate as possible, is so unfavorable that as far as it can judge in advance with something close to certainty, the lily can predict that it will be snapped off at that very instant, so that its coming into existence becomes its downfall—indeed, so that it seems as if it only came into existence and became lovely in order to perish: the obedient lily submits to this obediently; it knows that such is God's will, and it springs forth. If you saw it at that moment there would not be the least indication that this unfolding was also its downfall; it sprang forth in such rich, beautiful fashion, so richly and beautifully did it go forth—for the whole thing was just a moment—it went to its downfall in unconditional obedience. In the lily's place, a human being, or we human beings, would certainly despair at the thought that coming into existence and downfall were one, and then in despair we would hinder

ourselves in becoming what we could have become, even if only for a moment. It is otherwise
with the lily; it was unconditionally obedient;
therefore it became itself in loveliness; it actually
became its entire possibility, undisturbed, unconditionally undisturbed, by the thought that that
very moment was its death. Ah, if one lily differed from another in its loveliness, this lily would
have to be awarded the prize: it possesses one
additional loveliness, to be lovely like this despite
the certainty of downfall at the same moment.
And truly, confronted with one's downfall, to
have the courage and the faith to come into existence in all one's loveliness: only unconditional
obedience is capable of this. As noted, the certainty of downfall would disturb a human being,
so that although only the briefest of existences
had been allotted him, he did not fulfill the possibility he had in fact been granted. "To what purpose?" he would say, or "Why?" he would say, or
"What good will it do?" he would say: and then
he would not develop the whole of his potential,
but would be culpable—crippled and unbeautiful
as he was—of having succumbed in advance of

55

the moment. Only unconditional obedience can encounter "the moment" unconditionally exactly; only unconditional obedience can make use of "the moment," unconditionally undisturbed by the next moment.

When the moment comes for it to depart, even though, according to its understanding of the matter, the bird is quite certain that things are quite good the way they are, and that to travel is thus to let go of what is certain in order to grasp what is uncertain, the obedient bird nonetheless immediately sets forth on the journey; in simple fashion and with the help of unconditional obedience, it understands only one thing but understands it unconditionally: that now is the moment, unconditionally.—When the bird comes into contact with the harshness of this life, when it is tried with difficulties and opposition, when, every morning, day after day, it finds that its nest has been disturbed: every day, the obedient bird begins its work all over again with the same joy and meticulousness it displayed the first time. In simple fashion and with the help of unconditional

obedience, it understands one thing, but understands it unconditionally: that this is its work and
that it is solely concerned with doing it.—When
the bird must experience the world's evil, when the
little songbird that sings to the glory of God must
put up with a naughty child's finding amusement
in jeering at it in order, if possible, to disturb the
solemnity; or when the solitary bird has found
surroundings it loves, a beloved branch on which
it especially loves to sit, perhaps also dear to it for
the most cherished memories—and then there is
a human being who takes delight in chasing it
away by throwing stones or in some other way—
alas, a human being who is just as untiring in evil
as the bird, despite having been driven off and
scared away, is untiring in returning to its love
and its old place: the obedient bird submits unconditionally to everything. In simple fashion
and with the help of unconditional obedience,
it understands only one thing, but understands it
unconditionally, that everything of this sort that
happens to it does not really concern it; that is,
these things only concern it in an unreal fashion,

or more correctly, that what actually concerns it—
but also unconditionally—is to submit to it in unconditional obedience to God.

So it is with the lily and the bird from whom
we should learn. Therefore, you must not say,
"The lily and the bird, of course they can be obedient; after all, they cannot do anything else or
they cannot do otherwise; to become an example
of obedience in that way is of course to make a
virtue of necessity." You are not to say anything
of this sort; you are to say nothing whatever. You
are to keep silent and obey, so that if it is indeed
true that the lily and the bird make a virtue of
necessity, you might also succeed in making a
virtue of necessity. You, too, are of course subject
to necessity. God's will is indeed done in any case,
so strive to make a virtue of necessity by doing
God's will in unconditional obedience. God's will
is indeed done in any case, so see to it that you
make a virtue of necessity by submitting to God's
will unconditionally obediently, so unconditionally
obediently that in connection with carrying out
and submitting to God's will, you might truth-

fully be able to say of yourself : "I cannot do anything else, I cannot do otherwise."

This is what you should strive for, and you
should consider that whatever the situation is with
the lily and the bird, if it actually is more difficult
for a human being to be unconditionally obedient, there is also a danger for the human being, a
danger that might, if I dare say so, make it easier
for him: the danger of forfeiting God's patience.
For have you ever truly earnestly examined your
own life, or examined human life, or the human
world—which is so different from that of nature,
where everything is unconditionally obedient—
have you ever considered this, and have you then
perceived, without shuddering, how much truth
there indeed is in God's calling himself "the God
of patience"; have you perceived that he, the God
who says "either/or"—understood as meaning,
"either love me or hate me, either hold fast to me
or despise me"—that he has the patience to bear
with you and me and with all of us! If God were
a human being, what then? Long, long ago he
would have to have become sick and tired of me

(to take myself as an example) and of having any-thing to do with me, and he would have to have said what human parents say (though for very different reasons): "The child is naughty and sickly and stupid and slow-witted, and if there were only something good about it, but there is so much bad about it—no human being can endure it." No, no human being can endure it, only the God of patience can do it.

And now think of the countless number of human beings who are living! We human beings speak of it as a task of patience to be a schoolmaster for little children. And now God, who has to be the schoolmaster for this countless number—what patience! And what makes the requirement of patience infinitely greater is that where God is the schoolmaster, more or less all the children suffer from the delusion that they are big, grown-up people, a delusion of which the lily and the bird are so entirely free that it is surely for this very reason that unconditional obedience comes so easily to them. "The only thing lacking," a human schoolmaster would say, "the only thing lacking would be for the children to imagine that they were grown-up people; then one would have to lose patience and despair; no human being could endure that." No, no human being could endure that; only the God of patience can do it. You see, that is why God calls himself the God of patience. And he certainly knows what he is saying. It is not when he is in a mood that it occurs to him to call himself this; no, he does not vary in mood; that would of course be impatience. He knew from eternity—and he knows from thousands upon thousands of years of daily experience—he knew from eternity that as long as temporality lasts, and human beings with it, he must be the God of patience, for otherwise human disobedience would be unendurable. In relating to the lily and the bird, God is the fatherly Creator and Sustainer; only in relation to human beings is he the God of patience. True enough, this is a consolation, an extremely necessary and indescribable consolation, which is in fact why scripture says that God is the God of patience—and "the God of consolation." But it is of course also a terribly serious matter that human disobedience is to blame for the fact that God is the God of patience, a terribly serious matter that human beings not take this patience in vain. Human beings discovered an attribute of God that the lily and the bird, who are always unconditionally obedient, do not know; or God had such love for human beings that he let it be revealed to them that he has this attribute, that he is patience. But thus in a certain sense—oh, frightful responsibility!—God's patience corresponds to human disobedience. This is a consolation, but subject to a terrible responsibility. A human being needs to know that even if all human beings gave up on him, indeed, even if he were on the verge of giving up on himself, God is still the God of patience. This is incalculable wealth. Ah, but make proper use of it; remember that it is your savings. For the sake of God in Heaven, use it properly; otherwise it plunges you into even greater wretchedness; it transforms itself into its opposite—it is no longer consolation, but becomes the most terrible of all accusations against you. For, if this seems to you to be too hard a saying (even though it is no harder than the truth is): that to fail to hold fast to God unconditionally and in everything—that this is "immediately" to despise him—then it certainly cannot be too hard a saying that to take God's patience in vain is to despise him!

Therefore, take great care to learn obedience from the lily and the bird in accordance with the gospel's instruction. Do not let yourself be frightened away; do not despair when you compare your life with the life of these teachers. There is nothing to despair over, for indeed you *shall* learn from them; and the gospel consoles you, first, by telling you that God is the God of patience, but then it adds: "You shall learn from the lily and the bird, learn to be unconditionally obedient like the lily and the bird, learn not to serve two masters, for no one can serve two masters, he must either … or."

But if you can become unconditionally obedient like the lily and the bird, you have learned what you should have learned, and you have learned it from the lily and the bird (and if you have learned it thoroughly, you have in this way become the more perfect one, so that the lily and the bird, from having been the teachers, become the metaphor); you have learned to serve only one

master, to love him alone, and to hold fast to him
unconditionally in everything. Then, the prayer
(which, it is true, will be fulfilled in any case)
would be fulfilled by you when you pray to God:
"Your will be done on earth as it is in heaven," for
in unconditional obedience, your will is indeed
one with God's will, and thus God's will is done
through you on earth as it is in heaven. And then
your prayer, when you pray, "Lead us not into
temptation," will also be heard, for if you are
unconditionally obedient to God, then there is
nothing ambivalent in you, and if there is nothing ambivalent in you, then you are sheer simplicity before God. But there is one thing that all
Satan's cunning and all the snares of temptation
cannot take by surprise or take captive: it is simplicity. That for which Satan keeps a sharp-eyed
lookout as his prey (but that is never found in the
lily and the bird), that at which all temptation
aims, certain of its prey (but that is never found
in the lily and the bird)—is ambivalence. Where
there is ambivalence, there temptation *is*, and it is
only altogether too easily the stronger there. But
where ambivalence is, in one way or another, deep

down there is also disobedience. There is nothing whatever ambivalent in the lily and the bird precisely because unconditional obedience is present deep down and everywhere; and it is precisely for this reason, because there is nothing ambivalent in the lily and the bird, that it is impossible to lead the lily and the bird into temptation. Where there is no ambivalence, Satan is powerless; where there is no ambivalence, temptation is as powerless as a bird catcher with his snares when there are no birds to be found. But just the least little glint of the ambivalence, then Satan is strong and the temptation is captivating; and he is sharp-eyed, he the evil one whose snare is called temptation and whose prey is called a person's soul. Temptation does not actually come from him, but nothing, nothing ambivalent can conceal itself from him; and if he discovers this, temptation is allied with him. But the person who conceals himself in God in unconditional obedience is unconditionally secure; from his secure hiding place he can see the devil, but the devil cannot see him. From his secure hiding place—for, as sharp-eyed as the devil is when it comes to ambivalence, he is

65

equally blind when he looks upon simplicity—he becomes blind or is stricken with blindness. Yet the unconditionally obedient person does not look upon the devil without shuddering—that glittering gaze that looks as if it could penetrate heaven and earth and the most hidden recesses of the heart, as it indeed can—and yet, that he with this gaze, that he should be blind! But if he who sets the trap of temptation—if he is blind with respect to the person who conceals himself in God with unconditional obedience—then, for that person there is indeed no temptation, for "God tempts no one." Thus his prayer has been heard: "Lead us not into temptation"—that is, let me never, ever disobediently stray from my hiding place, and if I am indeed guilty of disobedience, then do not immediately expel me from my hiding place, outside of which I am immediately led into temptation. And if he then remains in his hiding place in unconditional obedience, he is also "delivered from evil."

No one can serve two masters; he must either love the one and hate the other, or hold fast to the one and despise the other. You cannot serve God and mammon, not God and the world, not good and evil. Thus, there are two powers: God and the world, good and evil, and the reason a human being can only serve one master is certainly that these two powers—even though one power is infinitely stronger than the other—are in mortal combat with one another. This enormous danger— a danger in which a human being is indeed situated by virtue of being a human being, a danger that the lily and the bird are spared in their unconditional obedience, which is happy innocence, for neither God and the world nor good and evil are fighting over them—this enormous danger, that "the human being" is situated between these two enormous powers and the choice is left to him: this enormous danger is that one must either love or hate, that not to love is to hate, for these two powers are so hostile that the least inclination to one side is regarded by the other side as unconditional opposition. If a human being forgets this absolute danger in which he is situated (and, note well, the attempt to forget a danger of this sort is certainly no useful protection against it)—if a human being forgets that he is situated in this enormous danger, if he believes he is not in danger, if he even says, "Peace and no danger," then the words of the gospel must seem to him a foolish exaggeration. Alas, precisely because he is so sunken in danger and is lost, he has neither any notion of the love with which God loves him and that it is precisely out of love that God requires unconditional obedience, nor has he any notion of the power and cunning of evil and of his own weakness. And from the very first, a human being is too childish to be able to understand the gospel and to want to do so; its talk of either/or seems to him an untrue exaggeration: that the danger should be so great, that unconditional obedience should be required, that the requirement of unconditional obedience should be grounded in love—a human being cannot get this into his head.

What, then, does the gospel do? The gospel, which is the wisdom of upbringing, does not get involved in an intellectual or verbal quarrel with a person in order to *prove* to him that it is so; the gospel knows very well that this is not the way things are done, that a human being does not first understand that what it says is so and then decide to obey unconditionally, but the reverse, that only by unconditionally obeying does a human being come to understand that what the gospel says is so. Therefore the gospel makes use of authority and says: "You *shall*." But at the same moment it becomes gentler, so that it might be capable of moving even the hardest heart; it takes you by the hand, as it were—and does just as the loving father does with his child—and says: "Come, let us go out to the lily and the bird." Out there, it continues by saying: "Consider the lilies of the field; abandon yourself to them, lose yourself in them—does not this sight move you?" Then, when the solemn silence out there with the lily and the bird moves you deeply, the gospel explains fur-ther, saying: "But why is this silence so solemn? Because it expresses the unconditional obedience with which everything serves only one master, turns in service only toward one, joined in complete unity, in one great divine service—so let yourself be gripped by this great thought, for it is all only one thought, and learn from the lily and the bird." But do not forget, you *shall* learn from the lily and the bird; you shall become unconditionally obedient like the lily and the bird. Consider that it was the sin of a human being that—by being unwilling to serve one master, or by wanting to serve another master, or by wanting to serve two, indeed, many masters—disturbed the beauty of the whole world where previously everything had been so very good; it was his sin that introduced discord into a world of unity; and consider that every sin is disobedience and every disobedience is sin.

III

"LOOK AT THE BIRDS OF
THE AIR; THEY NEITHER
SOW NOR REAP NOR
GATHER INTO BARNS"—
*UNCONCERNED ABOUT
TOMORROW.* "CONSIDER
THE GRASS OF THE
FIELD—*WHICH TODAY IS.*"

Do THIS and learn:

joy.

So let us then consider the lily and the bird, these joyful teachers. "The joyful teachers," indeed, because you know that joy is communicative, and therefore no one teaches joy better than a person who is joyful himself. The teacher of joy really has nothing other to do than to be joyful himself, or to be joy. However much he strains to communicate

71

joy—if he himself is not joyful, the instruction is imperfect. Thus, nothing is easier to teach than joy—alas, one needs only to be truly joyful oneself. But alas, this "alas" means that this is in fact not so easy—that is, it is not so easy always to be joyful oneself, for it is easy enough to teach joy when one is joyful: nothing is more certain than that.

But out there with the lily and the bird, or out there where the lily and the bird teach joy, there is always joy. And the lily and the bird never find themselves in an embarrassing position as sometimes happens to a human teacher when he has written his teaching notes on a sheet of paper or has them among his books, in short, somewhere else and not always with him; no, *there*, where the lily and the bird teach joy, there is always joy— it is, after all, within the lily and the bird. What joy, when day is dawning and the bird awakens early to the joy of the day; what joy, even though in another key, when the dusk is falling and the bird hastens home to its nest; and what joy, the long summer day! What joy, when the bird—not merely like a joyful worker who sings at his work, but whose essential work is singing—joyfully begins his song. What new joy, when his neighbor, too, begins, and then the neighbor across the way, and when the whole chorus joins in, what joy. And when, finally, it is like a sea of sound that makes the forest, the valley, the sky, and the earth resound, a sea of sound in which the bird that sounded the opening note now frolics with joy: what joy, what joy! And so it is throughout the bird's entire life: everywhere and always it finds something—or, better, it finds enough—in which to take joy. It does not waste a single moment, but it would view as wasted every moment in which it was not joyful.—What joy, when the dew falls and refreshes the lily, which has now cooled off and prepares to rest; what joy, when after its bath the lily sensually dries itself in the first ray of sunlight; and what joy, the long summer day! Ah, just consider them. Consider the lily; consider the bird; and look at them together! What joy, when the bird hides behind the lily, where it has its nest and where it is so indescribably cozy, while it passes the time in jesting and bantering with the lily! What joy when high up from the branch, or

higher up, all the way up in the cloud, the bird
blissfully keeps its eye on its nest and on the lily
which smilingly turns its eye up toward it! Bliss-
ful, happy existence, so rich in joys! Or is the joy
perhaps lesser because, narrowly understood, it
takes so little to give them such joy? No, this
narrow-minded understanding is indeed surely a
misunderstanding, alas, an extremely deplorable
and lamentable misunderstanding; for the very
fact that what gives them such joy is so little is
proof that they themselves are joy and joy itself.
But is this truly so? If what one rejoiced over was
nothing at all, and yet one truly was indescribably
joyful, this would be the best proof that one is
oneself joy and joy itself—as are the lily and the
bird, the joyful teachers of joy, who, precisely because they are *unconditionally joyful*, are joy itself.
For example, the person whose joy is dependent
upon certain conditions is not himself joy; his joy,
after all, is that of the conditions and is conditional upon them. But a person who is joy itself
is unconditionally joyful, just as, conversely, the
person who is unconditionally joyful is joy itself.
Oh, the conditions for becoming joyful cause us

74

human beings much trouble and concern—even if all the conditions were fulfilled, we perhaps would not become unconditionally joyful anyway. But, you profound teachers of joy, is it not true that it indeed cannot be otherwise, because with the help of conditions—even of all the conditions—it is of course impossible to become more or other than conditionally joyful; indeed, the conditions and that which is subject to conditions correspond to one another. No, only the person who is joy itself becomes unconditionally joyful, and only by becoming unconditionally joyful does one become joy itself.

But could one not indicate quite briefly how joy is the content of the lily's and the bird's instruction, or what is the content of this instruction of theirs in joy—that is, could one not indicate quite briefly the thought categories of this instruction of theirs? Yes, that can be easily done, for however simple the lily and the bird are, they are not thoughtless. So it can be easily done; and in this connection let us not forget that we already have an extraordinary shortcut: the lily and the bird are themselves what they teach; they themselves express the subject in which they give instruction as teachers. This is different from the straightforward and primal originality, that in the strictest sense the lily and the bird possess firsthand that which they teach—it is acquired originality. And of course this acquired originality in the lily and the bird is in turn simplicity, for whether instruction is simple does not depend so much on the use of simple, everyday expressions or high-flown, learned language—no, simplicity is that the teacher himself is what he teaches. And so it is in the case of the lily and the bird. But their instruction in joy, which is in turn expressed by their lives, is quite briefly as follows: There is a today; it *is*. Indeed, an infinite emphasis is placed upon this *is*. There is a today—and there is no worry, absolutely none, about tomorrow or the day after tomorrow. This is not foolishness on the part of the lily and bird, but is the joy of silence and obedience. For when you keep silent in the solemn silence of nature, then tomorrow does not exist, and when you obey as a creature obeys, then there exists no tomorrow, that unfortunate day that is the invention of garrulousness and disobedience. But when, owing to silence and obedience, tomorrow does not exist, then, in the silence and obedience, today is, it *is*—and then the joy is, as it is in the lily and the bird.

What is joy, or what is it to be joyful? It is truly to be present to oneself; but truly to be present to oneself is this "today," this to *be* today, truly to *be today*. And the truer it is that you *are* today, the more you are entirely present to yourself in being today, the less does tomorrow, the day of misfortune, exist for you. Joy is the present time, with the entire emphasis falling on *the present time*. Therefore God is blessed, he who eternally says: "Today," he who is eternally and infinitely present to himself in being today. And therefore the lily and the bird are joy, because by silence and unconditional obedience they are entirely present to themselves in being today.

"But," you say, "the lily and the bird, of course they can." Reply: You must not come with any "But"—but learn from the lily and the bird to be entirely present to yourself in being today, as they are; then you, too, are joy. But, as has been said, no "But," for this is in earnest: You *shall* learn joy

from the lily and the bird. Even less may you become self-important—in view of the fact that the
lily and the bird, after all, are simple—so that
you (perhaps in order to feel that you are a human
being) become clever, and speaking with reference to some particular tomorrow, say: "The lily
and the bird, of course they can—they who do
not even have a tomorrow by which to be plagued,
but a human being, who of course not only has
worries about tomorrow, about what he is to eat,
but also about yesterday, about what he has
eaten—and not paid for!" No, no witticism that
impudently disturbs the instruction. But learn, at
least begin to learn, from the lily and the bird.
For of course no one can seriously believe that
what the lily and bird rejoice over, and similar
things—are nothing to rejoice over! Thus, that you
came into existence, that you exist, that "today"
you receive the necessities of existence, that you
came into existence, that you became a human
being, that you can see—consider this: that you
can see, that you can hear, that you have a sense
of smell, that you have a sense of taste, that you
can feel; that the sun shines for you and for your

sake, that when it becomes weary, the moon begins to shine and the stars are lit; that it becomes
winter, that all of nature disguises itself, pretends
to be a stranger—and does so in order to delight
you; that spring comes, that birds come in large
flocks—and do so in order to bring you joy; that
green plants spring forth, that the forest grows
into beauty, has its nuptials—and does so in order
to bring you joy; that autumn comes, that the
birds fly away, not to make themselves precious
and hard to get, oh, no, but so that you will not
become bored with them; that the forest puts
away its finery for the sake of the next time, that
is, so it can give you joy the next time: Is this
supposed to be nothing to rejoice over! Oh, if
I dared to scold—but out of respect for the lily
and the bird, I dare not—and therefore, instead
of saying that there is nothing to rejoice over, I
will say: If this is nothing to rejoice over, then
there is nothing over which to rejoice. Consider
that the lily and the bird are joy, and yet, understood in this manner, they of course have much
less to rejoice over than you do—you, who of
course also have the lily and the bird over which

79

to rejoice. Therefore, learn from the lily and learn from the bird, who are the teachers: who exist, who *are today*, and who *are* joy. If you cannot look with joy upon the lily and the bird, who of course are joy itself, if you cannot look upon them with joy so that you become willing to learn from them: then your case is like that of the child of whom the teacher says: "It is not lack of ability— furthermore, the material is so easy that there can be no question of lack of ability—it must be something else, though perhaps only an indisposition, which one must not be overhasty in judging too strictly, treating it as unwillingness or, indeed, as rebelliousness."

Thus the lily and the bird are teachers of joy. And yet the lily and the bird of course also have cares or sorrows as all of nature has sorrows. Does not all of creation sigh under the perishability to which it has been subjected against its will? It is all subjected to perishability! A star, however firmly it is fixed in the heavens—indeed, the one most firmly fixed—shall nevertheless change its place in the fall, and the one that never changed its position shall nevertheless one day change its position when it plunges into the abyss. And the whole of this world, with everything that is in it, shall be changed as one changes a garment when it is discarded, the prey of perishability! And even if it escapes the fate of being immediately cast into the oven, the lily must nevertheless wither after having already suffered one thing and another. And even if it were permitted to die of old age, at some point the bird must nevertheless die, separated from its beloved, after having already suffered one thing and another. Oh, it is all perishability, and everything will at some point become what it is, the prey of perishability. Perishability, perishability, that is *the sigh*—for to be subjected to perishability is to be what a sigh signifies: confinement, incarceration in prison; and the content of the sigh is: perishability, perishability!

Yet the lily and the bird are unconditionally joyful; and here you can properly see how true it is when the gospel says: "You *shall* learn joy from the lily and the bird." For of course you cannot require any better teacher than the one who, despite the fact that he bears so infinitely deep a sorrow, is nonetheless unconditionally joyful and is joy itself.

How, then, do the lily and the bird manage this, which almost looks like a miracle: in deepest sorrow to be unconditionally joyful; when it is so frightful tomorrow, then to *be*, that is, to be unconditionally joyful today—how do they manage it? They manage it quite plainly and simply— as the lily and the bird always do—and yet they get rid of this tomorrow as if it did not exist. There is a saying by the apostle Paul that the lily and the bird have taken to heart and, simple as they are, they take it quite literally—ah, and precisely this, taking it quite literally, is what helps them.[1] These words have enormous power when they are taken quite literally; when they are not taken literally, exactly according to the letter, they are more or less powerless, finally merely a mean-

1   Kierkegaard subsequently realized that his reference here to "the apostle Paul" was erroneous. In journal entry NB11:168, from the early summer of 1849, Kierkegaard wrote, "It is rather odd that in the *Three Godly Discourses*, I ascribed Peter's 'cast all you sorrows on God' to Paul" (Bruce H. Kirmmse et al., eds. and trans., *Kierkegaard's Journals and Notebooks* [Princeton, NJ: Princeton University Press, 2012], vol. 6, p. 95). See 1 Pet 5:7.

ingless figure of speech; but unconditional simplicity is required in order to take them unconditionally altogether literally. "Cast **all** your care or sorrow **upon God**." See, the lily and the bird do this unconditionally. With the help of unconditional silence and unconditional obedience, they cast—indeed, as the most powerful catapult casts something away from itself, and with a passion like that with which a person casts away what he most detests—**all** their sorrow away and cast it— with a sureness like that with which the most reliable of guns hits its mark, and with a faith and confidence like that one encounters only in the most practiced marksman—**upon God**. At that very instant—and this very instant is from the first moment, is today, is contemporaneous with the first moment it exists—at that very instant it is unconditionally joyful. Marvelous dexterity! To be able to take hold of all one's sorrow at once, and then to be able to cast it away from oneself so dexterously and hit the mark with such certainty! Yet this is what the lily and the bird do, and therefore they are unconditionally joyful at that very instant. And of course this is entirely in order, for God the Almighty bears the whole world and all the world's sorrow—including the lily's and the bird's—with infinite lightness. What indescribable joy! Joy, namely, over God the Almighty.

So learn, then, from the lily and the bird, learn this, the dexterity of the unconditioned. True enough, it is a marvelous feat, but that is precisely the reason why you must pay attention all the more closely to the lily and the bird. It is a marvelous feat and, like "the feat of meekness," it contains a contradiction, or it is a feat that resolves a contradiction. The word "cast" leads one to think of the use of force, as if one ought to gather all one's strength and with an enormous exercise of strength—forcibly "cast" the sorrow away—and yet, yet "force" is precisely what is not to be used. What is to be used, and used unconditionally, is "compliance"—and yet one is to "cast" sorrow away! And one is to cast "all" sorrow away; if one does not cast *all* sorrow away, then one of course retains much of it, some of it, a little of it—one does not become joyful; even less does one become unconditionally joyful. And if one does not cast it unconditionally *upon God* but somewhere else, then one is not unconditionally rid of it; then, one way or another, it comes back again, most often in the form of an even greater and more bitter sorrow. For to cast sorrow away, but not upon God, is "distraction." But distraction is a dubious and ambivalent remedy for sorrow. On the other hand, unconditionally to cast all sorrow upon God is "collectedness," and yet— yes, amazingly, this is the feat performed by this contradiction!—a *collectedness* through which you unconditionally *get rid of* all sorrow.

Learn, then, from the lily and the bird. Cast all your sorrow upon God! But you shall not cast away joy; on the contrary, you shall hold fast to it with all your might and all your vital strength. If you do this, then the reckoning is easily done: you will always retain some joy. For if you cast away all sorrow, you of course retain only whatever joy you have. Yet this will avail but little. Learn, therefore, from the lily and the bird. Cast all your sorrow upon God, entirely, unconditionally, as the lily and the bird do: then you will become unconditionally joyful like the lily and the bird. It is, namely, unconditional joy to worship the omnipotence with which God the Almighty bears all your sorrow as lightly as nothing. And the next thing (which the apostle indeed adds) is also unconditional joy: in worshipping, to dare to believe "that God cares for you." Unconditional joy is precisely joy over God, over whom and in whom you can always unconditionally rejoice. If you do not become unconditionally joyful in this situation, the fault lies unconditionally in you, in your clumsiness in casting all your sorrow upon him, in your unwillingness to do so, in your conceitedness, in your stubbornness—in short, it lies in your not being like the lily and the bird. There is only one sorrow with respect to which the lily and the bird cannot be the teacher, a sorrow of which we therefore will not speak here: the sorrow of sin. With respect to all other sorrows, it is the case that if you do not become unconditionally joyful, the fault is yours for not wanting to learn from the lily and the bird to become unconditionally joyful over God through unconditional silence and obedience.

Yet one more thing. Perhaps, with "the poet," you say: "Yes, if one could build and live alongside the bird, concealed in the solitude of the forest, where the bird and its mate are a pair, but where there otherwise is no society; or if one could live together with the lily in the peace of the field, where every lily looks after itself and where there is no society: then one could certainly cast all one's sorrow upon God and be or become unconditionally joyful. For 'society,' society itself, causes the problem that the human being is the only being that plagues itself and others with the ill-starred delusion about society and the bliss of society, and all the more so as society—to his and society's own depravity—becomes greater." You must not speak like this, however; no, consider the matter more closely and admit, to your shame, that despite the sorrow, there is actually an inexpressible joy of love with which the birds, male and female, are a pair, and that despite the sorrow, there is in the single state a self-contented joy with which the lily is solitary: that actually it is this joy that keeps them from being disturbed by society; for after all, society is there. Consider the situation still more closely and admit, to your shame, that indeed it is actually the unconditional silence

and the unconditional obedience with which the
bird and the lily are unconditionally joyful over
God—that this is actually what makes the lily
and the bird just as joyful, and just as unconditionally joyful, in solitude as in society. So learn,
then, from the lily and the bird.

And if you could learn to be entirely like the
lily and the bird: ah, and if I could learn it, then
the prayer would also be truth in you as in me,
the last prayer in "The Prayer," which (as an example for all true prayer, which of course prays
itself joyful and more joyful and unconditionally
joyful) in the end has nothing, nothing more to
pray for or to desire, but, unconditionally joyful,
ends in praise and worship, the prayer: "Yours is
the kingdom and the power and the glory." Yes,
his is the kingdom, and therefore *you* must unconditionally keep silent lest you direct disturb-
ing attention at the fact of your existence—but
through the solemnity of unconditional silence
express that the kingdom is his. And *his* is the
power, and therefore you must unconditionally
obey and be unconditionally obedient in submitting to everything, for his is the power. And *his* is

the glory, and therefore in everything you do and everything you suffer you have unconditionally one more thing to do, to give him the glory, for the glory is his.

Oh, unconditional joy: his is the kingdom and the power and the glory—forever. "Forever"— behold, this day, the day of eternity, it indeed never comes to an end. Therefore, only hold unconditionally fast to this: that his is the kingdom and the power and the glory forever; then there is for you a "today" that never ends, a today in which you can eternally remain present to yourself. Then let the heavens fall and the stars change their places in the overturning of everything, let the bird die and the lily wither: *this very day* your joy in worship, and you in your joy, will nevertheless survive every destruction. Consider what concerns you, if not as a human being, then as a Christian: that from a Christian standpoint even the danger of death is so insignificant to you that it is said: "*this very day* you are in paradise." And thus the transition from time to eternity—the greatest possible distance—is so swift that even if it were to take place through the destruction of everything, you are in paradise *this very day*, because from a Christian standpoint, you *abide in God*. For if you abide in God, then whether you live or die, whether things go well or badly for you while you are alive; whether you die today or only after seventy years; and whether you find your death at the bottom of the sea, at its greatest depth, or you are exploded in the air: you still do not come to be outside of God, you *abide*—thus you remain present to yourself in God and therefore on the day of your death you are in paradise this very day. The bird and the lily live only one day, and a very short day, and yet are joy because, as has been shown, they genuinely *are **today***, are *present to themselves* in this "today." And you, to whom the longest day is granted: to live today—and this very day to be in paradise—should you not be unconditionally joyful, you who even should, since indeed you could, far, far surpass the bird in joy? This is something you are assured of every time you pray this prayer, and something to which you also draw near every time you fervently pray this prayer of joy: "Yours is the kingdom and the power and the glory—forever, Amen."